The Explosive Child

THE WORKBOOK

Disclaimer:

The information in this workbook provides guidance for understanding and managing explosive behavior in children, but individual results may vary as each child is unique. Strategies and techniques are based on general principles and research, but professional help and personalized guidance should be considered. The chapters offer insights on understanding explosive behavior, collaborative problem-solving, dealing with explosive behavior, helping develop self-control, and the power of persistence. However, consulting professionals is crucial, as the strategies may not address all underlying causes, and progress may require time and setbacks may occur. This workbook does not replace professional advice, and the authors disclaim liability for any damages arising from its use.

Thank you for choosing to engage with this book. We hope it helps you build a healthy and loving relationship with your partner.

LESSONS IN THIS WORKBOOK:

Chapter 1: Understanding Explosive Behavior

Lesson 1:

Explosive children are often misunderstood. They are not bad or defiant; they are simply struggling to cope with frustration.

Reflect on a recent incident where a child's explosive behavior was misinterpreted or misunderstood. Write a journal entry describing the factors that may have contributed to the misunderstanding. Explore the emotions and thoughts that arose as a result. Reflect on how a shift in perspective can help cultivate empathy and understanding.

Write a letter to a parent or caregiver of an explosive child, offering support and understanding. Share your insights on the nature of explosive behavior and emphasize that it is not a reflection of a child's character. Provide examples or anecdotes to illustrate this point and offer words of encouragement to the parent or caregiver.

Imagine yourself in the shoes of an explosive child. Write a narrative or story from their perspective, describing a frustrating situation that leads to an outburst. Reflect on the emotions and challenges they might experience and consider how this exercise can foster empathy and compassion.

Lesson 2:

Traditional parenting methods, such as punishment and rewards, often do not work with explosive children.

Reflect on your own experiences or observations with traditional parenting methods. Write a journal entry exploring situations where punishment or rewards may not have been effective in managing explosive behavior. Consider the potential reasons why these methods may fall short and how they may impact the child's emotional well-being.

Write a list of alternative approaches to discipline and behavior management that do not rely solely on punishment or rewards. Include strategies such as empathy, problem-solving, and collaboration. Reflect on how these approaches can better support explosive children and promote positive behavior.

Choose a specific scenario involving an explosive child and create a hypothetical plan that avoids punishment and rewards. Write down the steps you would take to address the situation, focusing on problem-solving and understanding the underlying causes of the behavior. Reflect on how this alternative approach may lead to a more positive outcome.

_____

_____

_____

_____

_____

_____

_____

_____

_____

_____

_____

_____

_____

_____

_____

_____

_____

_____

_____

_____

_____

_____

_____

_____

Lesson 3:

A more effective approach is to focus on helping explosive children understand and solve the problems that lead to their outbursts.

Reflect on a recent incident where an explosive child had an outburst. Write a journal entry describing the potential underlying problems or triggers that may have contributed to the behavior. Explore possible solutions or strategies that could have helped the child understand and address those problems.

Write a letter to an explosive child, offering guidance and support in problem-solving. Share your insights on the importance of understanding the problems that lead to outbursts and provide practical steps they can take to better manage their frustrations. Emphasize the value of seeking help and collaborating with others.

Create a problem-solving worksheet or template that can be used with an explosive child. Include sections for identifying the problem, brainstorming possible solutions, evaluating the pros and cons of each solution, and selecting the best course of action. Encourage the child to complete the worksheet when they face challenging situations to promote self-awareness and problem-solving skills.

_____

_____

_____

_____

_____

_____

_____

_____

_____

_____

_____

_____

_____

_____

_____

_____

_____

_____

_____

_____

_____

_____

_____

_____

_____

Chapter 2:
The Three Cs of Collaborative Problem Solving

Lesson 1:

Caring means listening to your child with empathy and understanding.

Write a reflection on a recent conversation with your child where you demonstrated caring and empathy. Describe the specific listening skills you used, such as active listening and reflecting back their feelings. Reflect on the impact of this approach on your child's response and the overall communication dynamic.

Write a letter to your child, expressing your commitment to caring and empathetic listening. Share specific instances where you may have fallen short in the past and your intentions to improve. Discuss the importance of creating a safe and supportive space for open communication and problem-solving.

Reflect on a challenging situation your child faced recently. Write down three open-ended questions you can ask your child to show empathy and understanding. Practice using these questions in future conversations to deepen your connection and demonstrate your caring approach.

_____

_____

_____

_____

_____

_____

_____

_____

_____

_____

_____

_____

_____

_____

_____

_____

_____

_____

_____

_____

_____

_____

_____

Lesson 2:

Competence means teaching your child the skills they need to solve problems on their own.

Reflect on a specific problem-solving skill that you believe would benefit your child. Write a journal entry exploring the importance of teaching this skill and how it can empower your child to solve problems independently. Consider practical ways you can introduce and reinforce this skill in your child's daily life.

_____

_____

_____

_____

_____

_____

_____

_____

_____

_____

_____

_____

_____

_____

_____

_____

_____

_____

_____

_____

_____

_____

_____

_____

_____

Write a step-by-step guide or checklist for teaching your child a specific problem-solving skill. Break it down into manageable tasks and identify opportunities in your child's routine to practice and reinforce the skill. Reflect on how this approach can build their competence and self-confidence.

Imagine a scenario where your child faces a problem that requires a particular skill. Write a role-play dialogue between you and your child, where you guide them through the problem-solving process using the skill you want to teach. Reflect on the potential challenges your child might encounter and how you can provide guidance and support.

Lesson 3:

Control means giving your child choices and allowing them to make mistakes.

Reflect on a recent situation where you provided your child with choices. Write a journal entry describing the choices you offered and the impact it had on your child's behavior and decision-making. Reflect on the importance of autonomy and how providing choices can foster independence and learning.

_____

_____

_____

_____

_____

_____

_____

_____

_____

_____

_____

_____

_____

_____

_____

_____

_____

_____

_____

_____

_____

_____

_____

_____

_____

_____

Write a list of potential choices you can offer your child in various situations. Include both everyday scenarios and problem-solving situations. Reflect on how these choices can promote responsibility, ownership, and learning from mistakes.

Reflect on a specific mistake your child made and how you responded to it. Write a letter to your child, acknowledging the mistake and expressing your belief in their ability to learn and grow from it. Share your intentions to provide guidance and support while also allowing them to experience the consequences of their actions. Discuss the importance of resilience and learning from mistakes.

_____

_____

_____

_____

_____

_____

_____

_____

_____

_____

_____

_____

_____

_____

_____

_____

_____

_____

_____

_____

_____

_____

_____

_____

Chapter 3:
The Four Steps of Collaborative Problem Solving

Lesson 1:

Meet with your child to discuss the problem.

Reflect on a recent problem or conflict that arose with your child. Write a journal entry describing the process of meeting with your child to discuss the problem. Reflect on the dynamics of the conversation, your approach to active listening, and your efforts to create a safe and non-judgmental space. Identify areas for improvement and strategies to enhance future problem-solving meetings.

_____

_____

_____

_____

_____

_____

_____

_____

_____

_____

_____

_____

_____

_____

_____

_____

_____

_____

_____

_____

_____

_____

_____

_____

_____

_____

_____

_____

Write a script or outline for a problem-solving meeting with your child. Include specific steps you will take to ensure effective communication, such as setting aside dedicated time, using active listening techniques, and demonstrating empathy. Consider how this structured approach can foster open dialogue and understanding.

Reflect on a challenging situation your child is currently facing. Write a letter to your child, expressing your desire to meet and discuss the problem together. Share your intentions to listen attentively and validate their feelings. Emphasize the importance of collaborative problem-solving and your commitment to finding a solution together.

Lesson 2:

Brainstorm a list of possible solutions.

Identify a problem or challenge that you and your child can brain-storm solutions for. Write a list of possible solutions, encouraging creativity and open-mindedness. Reflect on the range of options generated and how each solution addresses different aspects of the problem.

Choose a specific problem-solving scenario and create a mind map or visual diagram to brainstorm potential solutions. Use branches or bubbles to represent different solution ideas and their possible outcomes. Reflect on the advantages and disadvantages of each solution and how they align with your child's needs and goals.

Write a letter to yourself, reflecting on a past problem-solving situation where you successfully generated multiple solutions. Describe the process of brainstorming and the criteria you used to evaluate the options. Reflect on how this approach fostered collaboration and empowered your child to actively participate in finding a solution.

Lesson 3:

Choose a solution that both you and your child can agree on.

Reflect on a past problem-solving situation where reaching a mutual agreement was challenging. Write a journal entry exploring the potential barriers to agreement and the emotions that arose during the process. Reflect on how you can approach future decision-making situations to enhance collaboration and create win-win solutions.

_____

_____

_____

_____

_____

_____

_____

_____

_____

_____

_____

_____

_____

_____

_____

_____

_____

_____

_____

_____

_____

_____

_____

_____

Write a dialogue or script between you and your child, role-playing a situation where you discuss and negotiate a solution. Practice active listening, expressing your needs and concerns, and finding areas of compromise. Reflect on the strategies used to foster agreement and how you can implement them in real-life situations.

_____

_____

_____

_____

_____

_____

_____

_____

_____

_____

_____

_____

_____

_____

_____

_____

_____

_____

_____

_____

_____

_____

_____

Choose a specific problem-solving scenario and create a decision matrix or chart. List the potential solutions along one axis and the desired outcomes or criteria along the other axis. Rate each solution based on how well it meets each criterion. Reflect on how this approach can facilitate a collaborative decision-making process and empower your child to actively contribute to the solution.

_____

_____

_____

_____

_____

_____

_____

_____

_____

_____

_____

_____

_____

_____

_____

_____

_____

_____

_____

_____

_____

_____

_____

Chapter 4:
Dealing with Explosive Behavior

Lesson 1:

When your child is having an outburst, it is important to stay calm and avoid reacting emotionally.

Reflect on a recent situation where your child had an outburst and write a journal entry describing your own emotional response. Explore the challenges you faced in staying calm and identify the triggers that may have contributed to your reaction. Reflect on strategies you can employ to regulate your emotions in future instances.

_____

_____

_____

_____

_____

_____

_____

_____

_____

_____

_____

_____

_____

_____

_____

_____

_____

_____

_____

_____

_____

_____

_____

_____

Write a letter to yourself, offering encouragement and support in staying calm during your child's outbursts. Remind yourself of the importance of modeling emotional regulation and discuss specific self-care practices you can engage in to maintain a calm mindset.

Create a list of calming techniques or strategies that work well for you. Write down specific actions or practices you can employ when faced with a challenging situation involving your child's explosive behavior. Reflect on how implementing these techniques can help you stay calm and respond effectively.

Lesson 2:

Instead, try to focus on understanding why your child is upset and what you can do to help them calm down.

Reflect on a recent outburst your child had and write a journal entry exploring the possible underlying reasons for their behavior. Consider their perspective and any triggers or stressors that may have contributed to their upset. Reflect on how understanding the root causes can guide your approach in helping them calm down.

Write a letter to your child, expressing your desire to understand and support them during their moments of distress. Share your commitment to empathetic listening and discuss specific strategies you can use to create a safe space for them to express their emotions. Reflect on how this approach can help them feel heard and supported.

_____

_____

_____

_____

_____

_____

_____

_____

_____

_____

_____

_____

_____

_____

_____

_____

_____

_____

_____

_____

_____

_____

_____

Choose a specific challenging behavior or situation your child frequently encounters. Write a problem-solving plan that focuses on understanding their perspective and finding proactive ways to help them calm down. Identify triggers, potential solutions, and coping strategies that align with their needs. Reflect on the benefits of this approach for both you and your child.

_____

_____

_____

_____

_____

_____

_____

_____

_____

_____

_____

_____

_____

_____

_____

_____

_____

_____

_____

_____

_____

_____

_____

_____

_____

_____

Lesson 3:

It is also important to set clear limits and consequences for your child's behavior.

Reflect on your current approach to setting limits and consequences for your child's behavior. Write a journal entry exploring the effectiveness of your current strategies and any challenges you face in enforcing them consistently. Reflect on how you can refine your approach to ensure clear expectations and appropriate consequences.

_____

_____

_____

_____

_____

_____

_____

_____

_____

_____

_____

_____

_____

_____

_____

_____

_____

_____

_____

_____

_____

_____

_____

_____

Write a letter to yourself, outlining the specific limits and consequences you want to establish for your child's behavior. Describe the
rationale behind each limit and the corresponding consequences.
Reflect on how communicating and enforcing these boundaries can
contribute to a more structured and harmonious environment.

_____

_____

_____

_____

_____

_____

_____

_____

_____

_____

_____

_____

_____

_____

_____

_____

_____

_____

_____

_____

_____

_____

_____

Choose a specific behavior that requires clearer limits and consequences. Write a behavior plan that outlines the expectations, consequences, and potential rewards for your child. Consider involving your child in the development of this plan to encourage ownership and understanding. Reflect on how implementing this plan can create a more consistent and respectful dynamic in your relationship with your child.

_____

_____

_____

_____

_____

_____

_____

_____

_____

_____

_____

_____

_____

_____

_____

_____

_____

_____

_____

_____

_____

_____

_____

Chapter 5:
Helping Your Child Develop Self-Control

Lesson 1:

Self-control is the ability to manage your emotions and behavior in a way that is appropriate for the situation.

Reflect on a recent situation where you demonstrated self-control and write a journal entry describing the emotions and thoughts you experienced during that time. Explore how your ability to manage your emotions influenced your behavior and the outcome of the situation. Reflect on the importance of self-control in promoting positive interactions and relationships.

Write a letter to your child, sharing a personal story or anecdote that highlights the value of self-control. Discuss the positive outcomes that can result from managing emotions effectively and maintaining self-control. Encourage your child to reflect on their own experiences and identify instances where self-control could have led to a better outcome.

Write down a list of potential benefits that your child can experience by developing self-control. Reflect on how these benefits can positively impact their relationships, academic performance, and overall well-being. Encourage your child to add to the list and reflect on their own motivations for developing self-control.

Lesson 2:

There are a number of things you can do to help your child develop self-control.

Research and identify relaxation techniques that are suitable for children, such as deep breathing exercises or guided imagery. Write step-by-step instructions for a relaxation technique that you believe would be helpful for your child. Reflect on how practicing relaxation techniques can assist your child in managing their emotions and developing self-control.

_____

_____

_____

_____

_____

_____

_____

_____

_____

_____

_____

_____

_____

_____

_____

_____

_____

_____

_____

_____

_____

_____

_____

_____

Create a list of common challenging situations or triggers for your child's impulsive behavior. Write down coping skills or strategies that you can teach your child to help them navigate these situations more effectively. Reflect on how these coping skills can empower your child to make better choices and exercise self-control.

Reflect on positive role models in your child's life, such as family members, friends, or community figures. Write a letter to your child, discussing the qualities and behaviors that make these individuals positive role models for self-control. Encourage your child to identify their own role models and reflect on how they can emulate their behavior.

_____

_____

_____

_____

_____

_____

_____

_____

_____

_____

_____

_____

_____

_____

_____

_____

_____

_____

_____

_____

_____

_____

_____

_____

_____

_____

Lesson 3:

Teaching relaxation techniques, helping develop coping skills, and providing positive role models can all contribute to helping your child develop self-control.

Write a plan for incorporating relaxation techniques into your child's daily routine. Outline specific times or situations where they can practice these techniques and discuss how you can provide guidance and support. Reflect on how consistent practice can contribute to the development of self-control.

_____
_____
_____
_____
_____
_____
_____
_____
_____
_____
_____
_____
_____
_____
_____
_____
_____
_____
_____
_____
_____
_____
_____

Develop a set of coping skill cards or prompts that your child can refer to in challenging situations. Write down different coping strategies on individual cards and encourage your child to select and practice these skills when faced with triggers. Reflect on how equipping your child with coping skills can empower them to respond with self-control.

_____

_____

_____

_____

_____

_____

_____

_____

_____

_____

_____

_____

_____

_____

_____

_____

_____

_____

_____

_____

_____

_____

_____

_____

_____

_____

Create a collage or visual representation that showcases positive role models for self-control. Include pictures, quotes, or symbols that represent these individuals and their qualities. Display the collage in a prominent place as a reminder for your child of the importance of self-control and the potential positive impact it can have on their lives.

Chapter 6:
The Power of Persistence

Lesson 1:

It takes time and effort to help an explosive child learn new ways of coping.

Reflect on the progress you have made so far in helping your explosive child learn new coping strategies. Write a journal entry describing the specific techniques or interventions you have implemented and the impact they have had. Reflect on any challenges you have encountered and identify areas where you can dedicate more time and effort to support your child's growth.

_____

_____

_____

_____

_____

_____

_____

_____

_____

_____

_____

_____

_____

_____

_____

_____

_____

_____

_____

_____

_____

_____

_____

_____

Write a letter to your future self, expressing your commitment to persistence in helping your child. Describe the importance of consistency and ongoing effort in the process of teaching new coping skills. Discuss specific strategies or resources you plan to explore to enhance your child's development.

_____

_____

_____

_____

_____

_____

_____

_____

_____

_____

_____

_____

_____

_____

_____

_____

_____

_____

_____

_____

_____

_____

_____

_____

_____

_____

_____

Create a timeline or progress chart to track the milestones and achievements in your child's journey of learning new coping strategies. Write down the specific skills or behaviors you are targeting and include dates or checkpoints for evaluation. Reflect on the power of persistence as you observe the gradual progress and growth of your child.

_____

_____

_____

_____

_____

_____

_____

_____

_____

_____

_____

_____

_____

_____

_____

_____

_____

_____

_____

_____

_____

_____

_____

_____

Lesson 2:

It is important to be persistent and not give up.

Reflect on a specific challenging situation or setback you have en-countered while helping your explosive child. Write a journal entry exploring the emotions and thoughts that arose during that time. Discuss the potential reasons why you may have been tempted to give up and reflect on the impact of persistence in overcoming those challenges.

_____

_____

_____

_____

_____

_____

_____

_____

_____

_____

_____

_____

_____

_____

_____

_____

_____

_____

_____

_____

_____

_____

_____

_____

_____

Write a letter to your child, expressing your unwavering commitment to supporting them through their explosive behavior. Share stories of your own personal experiences with persistence and discuss how those experiences have shaped your understanding of its importance. Encourage your child to embrace resilience and persistence as they navigate their own challenges.

Identify potential barriers or obstacles that may hinder your persistence in helping your explosive child. Write down strategies or techniques you can employ to overcome these challenges. Reflect on the importance of self-care and seeking support from others to maintain your own motivation and persistence.

Lesson 3:

With time and patience, you can make a real difference in the life of your explosive child.

Reflect on the positive changes you have witnessed in your explosive child's life since you began your journey together. Write a journal entry describing the specific areas where you have seen progress and growth. Reflect on the impact these changes have had on your child's well-being and overall quality of life.

Write a letter to your child, expressing your belief in their potential for growth and transformation. Share specific examples of the positive changes you have observed in their behavior, emotions, or relationships. Encourage them to reflect on their own journey and the positive impact they have had on their own life and the lives of those around them.

Create a vision board or visual representation of the positive future you envision for your explosive child. Include images, quotes, or symbols that represent the growth, success, and well-being you hope for them. Display the vision board in a prominent place as a reminder of the potential and possibilities that lie ahead.

Made in the USA
Las Vegas, NV
07 November 2023

80422720R00044